# WITH EAGLE TAIL

ARNOLD LUPSON AND 30 YEARS AMONG THE SARCEE, BLACKFOOT AND STONEY
INDIANS ON THE NORTH AMERICAN PLAINS

COLIN F. TAYLOR AND HUGH DEMPSEY

SMITHMARK

# A SALAMANDER BOOK

This edition published in 1999 by SMITHMARK Publishers, a division of U.S. Media Holdings, Inc. 115 West 18th Street, New York, NY 10011.

SMITHMARK books are available for bulk purchase for sales promotion and premium use. For details write or call the manager of special sales, SMITHMARK Publishers, 115 West 18th Street, New York, NY 10011.

Produced by: Salamander Books Ltd.
8 Blenheim Court, Brewery Road, London N7 9NT, United Kingdom.

ISBN 0-7651-1059-8

Printed in Spain

1 0 9 8 7 6 5 4 3 2 1

Library of Congress Catalog Card Number: 98-75009

Editor: Polly Boyd
Designer: John Heritage
Filmset: SX Composing Ltd, England
Mono Reproduction: P & W Graphics, Singapore

All pictures from the Glenbow Museum Collection, Calgary.

**COLIN TAYLOR**      **ACKNOWLEDGEMENTS**

Travel to Alberta enabled me to confer with my friend Hugh Dempsey over the selection of Eagle Tail photographs and to extend studies of Sarcee, Stoney, and Blackfoot material culture at the Glenbow Museum collections and by visits to the reserves. I am grateful for the help from the Glenbow staff, the courtesies shown to me on the reserves and the hospitality of the Dempsey family. Thanks to Neilian Glass and Sally Barnes (grandniece of Eagle Tail) for supplying information on Arnold Lupson's early years. Special thanks also go to Betty Taylor who has done a great deal of work on this volume. In that respect she is another author.

**HUGH DEMPSEY**      **NOTE TO READERS**

Over the past twenty years, some Native groups in Canada have indicated dissatisfaction with the terms "Indian" and "tribe." Instead, they have encouraged the use of "First Nations," "Native Canadians," "Aboriginals," and "Indigenous Peoples." Some tribes have also encouraged the native names for themselves, so that the Blackfoot tribe has become the Siksika First Nation, the Sarcee are the Tsuu T'ina First Nation, and the Stoney the Nakoda First Nation. These terms have found varying degrees of acceptance in their own communities. Agencies such as The Department of Indian Affairs have kept their titles without being criticized. This book uses the terms which were in use during Eagle Tail's time. We hope readers will accept the use of these terms with their traditional meanings.

TITLE PAGE: *Lame Bull, an old-time warrior and buffalo hunter.*

PAGE 4: *A Sarcee camp in the 1930s with a wolf tepee in the foreground.*

# CONTENTS

# FOREWORD
## BY NEILIAN GLASS

I WAITED WITH mild interest for a lady by the name of Sally Barnes to arrive at my house. Sally had phoned me a couple of days earlier after hearing me talk on the radio about my research into Native American art and culture. She told me her great uncle, Arnold Lupson, had been a photographer who, in the early part of this century, had emigrated to Calgary and been adopted into the Sarcee Indian tribe. She had some of his photographs and thought I might like to see them. The reason for my lack of enthusiasm was that so many people have brought all sorts of "Indian" relics to show me. Unfortunately, they often turn out to have very dubious origins with equally dubious stories to go with them. I hoped that this was not going to be yet another.

SALLY ARRIVED carrying a plastic carrier bag and a small red carryall. We sat down and she drew an old photograph album from one of the bags and handed it to me. I opened the album and gazed on the first page of pictures, then the next page and the next. I knew immediately that these photographs were unique. I have seen many pictures of Native Americans and they almost always have the same stern, tense stiffness to them, the subjects uncomfortable with having their picture taken.

THE PEOPLE IN these photographs were relaxed, some going about their business or posing with friends or family. Even in the portrait-style pictures, the subjects look at ease and happy to be having their picture taken. The reason for this was that the photographer, although non-native, was a trusted friend, welcome in the homes of all the leading native families and a common sight on the reserve with his camera.

RIGHT: *One of the few automobiles to appear on the Sarcee Reserve in the 1930s was Eagle Tail's two-seater Ford. Eagle Tail lived in Calgary, about 8 miles (5km) from the little log cabin that he shared with Maggie Big Belly.*

THE PHOTOGRAPHS Sally had were ones Arnold Lupson had sent home to
his sister in Britain between 1914 and the mid-1950s. Sally was not
aware of the existence of any other photographs, but I was sure there
would be more. After a few telephone calls, I learned that there was a
collection of Lupson's photographs in the Glenbow Museum in

Neilian Glass

# INTRODUCTION
## BY HUGH DEMPSEY

THE TWENTY-FIVE-YEAR-OLD Englishman, Arnold Lupson, watched with fascination as the prairie Indians in their beaded costumes trotted by on their lavishly decorated horses. The occasion was the great Victory Stampede, held in Calgary, Alberta, to commemorate the end of the Great War. The Indians were the Sarcees, Blackfoot, and Stoneys who had been permitted to leave their reserves for this holiday celebration. This is what Lupson had traveled halfway around the world to see.

ARNOLD LUPSON WAS born in London in about 1895 and, according to one story, he was a photographer for the London *Daily Mirror* when he was assigned to take pictures of a group of Native Americans who were visiting England. Inspired by the experience, he decided to emigrate to Canada to see the native peoples in their own homeland. Upon arrival in Calgary in 1919, the only work available to the inexperienced young Englishman was in tanning hides for the Alberta Robe & Tannery Ltd. It was a dirty, smelly job but he gradually learned to handle all kinds of leather, and found it to be an ideal outlet for his artistic abilities. In 1922, he joined the large firm of Great West Saddlery as a warehouseman and was permitted to assist the artisans in the saddle-making shop. Within a year, he had been promoted to saddle maker and remained with the company for the next fifteen years.[1]

MEANWHILE, LUPSON'S skill as a photographer was soon demonstrated as he pursued his interest in Native American Indians. Each time there was a parade or other gathering, he was there with his camera, admiring the beaded dresses, feathered bonnets, and men's suits trimmed with

RIGHT: *Eagle Tail pauses in the early 1930s during construction of a house for his Sarcee wife, Maggie Big Belly. Her personal name was Searching Woman. Although Eagle Tail was not legally permitted to reside on the reserve, he spent much of his time there.*

horse hair or weasel skins. The people he saw fulfilled all his dreams and expectations of the "Red Indian of the Americas."

DURING THIS TIME, Lupson became friends with Joe Big Plume, head chief of the Sarcee tribe, whose reserve was on the southwestern outskirts of the city. Lupson was invited to visit the Big Plumes and got to know other families such as the Crow Childs, the Otters, and the Runners. He also was attracted to Joe Big Plume's sister, Maggie. She had become a widow in 1921 when her husband, former head chief Big Belly, had passed away. Her personal name was *Naditah'*, or Searching Woman. The chief noticed the friendly relationship between his sister and Lupson, and decided to do something about it. A Sarcee elder recalled, "That's how Lupson became involved with the Sarcees. He met Big Plume in Calgary, and they became friends. Later, Joe arranged for him to marry his younger sister in the traditional way. After Maggie became a widow, Joe convinced her that the white man would be able to look after her."[2]

AFTER HE STARTED with Great West Saddlery, Lupson took a small apartment downtown, close to where the Indians came to shop and meet their friends. On just about every weekend he visited the Sarcee Reserve and his wife, but he never lived there. Government regulations prevented this, and there were some Indians who always resented his presence and would have complained to the authorities if he had tried to become a permanent resident on the reserve. However, he did build a log house for Maggie and Mary, her daughter from the previous

ABOVE: *Eagle Tail and his wife, Maggie Big Belly, pose in their traditional Sarcee costumes. Eagle Tail has a fully beaded vest, beaded leggings, apron decorated with ribbons, and eagle feather headdress. His wife has a fully beaded yoke with an open basket-weave waist, beaded leggings, and moccasins.*

marriage, and stayed with them on weekends. "As it was," said the elder, "some people complained about him building the house and visiting the reserve, as they didn't want any white people on the reserve. But the Indian agent never did anything about it, as Joe Big Plume was [illegible]"[3]

[illegible]

Blackfoot, for example, called him [illegible] Eagle Tail. From the early 1920s, Eagle Tail began photographing southern Alberta Indians. He started with the Sarcees, and as his friends extended to other reserves, he added the Blackfoot, Bloods, Peigans, and Stoneys to his list. He concentrated on portraits, often taken in front of the subject's tepee, but did not miss the opportunity to include parades and other events. His first interest and love, however, remained the portraits. He emphasized the subject's buckskin and beaded costumes, and took pains to create an image of pride and haughty grandeur. Often he captured his subjects looking into an unfathomable distance, as though completely ignoring the presence of the camera. The result was to catch many prominent and respected people in poses that were unsurpassed by any other photographer in the area.

*the Sarcee tribe. He is seen here with Daisy Otter.*

EAGLE TAIL BECAME a familiar figure in the Indian village at the Calgary Stampede and at other gatherings, so he had no difficulty in attending Sun Dances, pow-wows, or celebrations held on the reserves. Although many Indians permitted him to take their picture, they were still wary about anyone recording their sacred rituals. This was based upon a belief that somehow a camera could rob a ceremony of its spiritual power. Only in a few instances was Eagle Tail able to record sacred rituals, most notably Sun Dances on the Blood and Blackfoot Reserves and a Medicine Pipe ceremony on the Sarcee.

IN 1923, HE PRODUCED a little booklet entitled *The Sarcee Indians of Alberta*, which has a picture of his brother-in-law on the cover and features ten large photographs of Sarcee Indians and an essay. The booklet is presented as "A short account of these people by a white man adopted into the tribe, who speaks their language and is acquainted with the many customs, beliefs and stories of this primitive people."[4] After briefly writing about Sarcee history and religion, Eagle Tail concludes, "In spite of the fact that these people live only eight miles from a city of 70,000 people, they cling tenaciously to their old customs. The medicine men still doctor the sick and their special ceremonies are performed each year as they have been for many hundreds of years past."[5]

EAGLE TAIL WAS described as a quiet and inoffensive man. He had his own beaded buckskin outfit and appeared to be a classic "wannabe."[6] He had a number of white friends but his closest companions over the years were Indians. He was remembered by the Sarcees as a non-smoker and a non-drinker, but he did have the reputation of pursuing Indian women and was said to have fathered at least one child on the

ABOVE: *Jack Big Plume, a Sarcee Indian, wears a coat, or capote, made from a Hudson's Bay Company blanket. He stands in front of a painted tepee decorated with bullrush, puffball, and mountain designs.*

Blackfoot Reserve. However, he and Maggie remained childless. He was also a thief, a fact admitted by both Indians and the police. In 1926, for example, he was arrested by the Calgary city police and served one month at hard labor for theft. On his arrest sheet, he was described as

stuff. He would go out with a ... no one was watching."[7]

EAGLE TAIL HAD no fear of retribution from angry spirits, for he was an avowed atheist. According to an elder, "Lupson was not a Christian and he didn't believe in the native religion. He used to make fun of all religions."[8] Another elder recalled, "He used to say he was an atheist, that he didn't believe in God, but after he died, we buried him in the Anglican cemetery on the reserve. I helped dig the grave. We were just finishing the funeral when a big storm came up, with hailstones the size of golf balls. It just pounded the earth on his grave and we had to run to a barn for shelter. We thought we were being punished for burying him in a Christian cemetery after he said he was an atheist."[9]

BESIDES BEING A photographer, Eagle Tail was also a collector of Indian artifacts and had a vision of someday opening his own museum. A step-grandson recalled that his rooms in downtown Calgary were covered with beadwork and other native objects. During the Great Depression of the 1930s, he often bought artifacts and beadwork from Sarcees who were in need of money. Also, because of his skill as a saddle maker, he would take orders from Indians and instead of money, he would trade a tooled leather saddle for a beaded dress or a man's buckskin outfit.

IN 1942, EAGLE TAIL quit Great West Saddlery and joined the firm of Adams Brothers Harnesses, where he was employed as a saddle maker but also had the freedom to make saddles on his own. He remained with them until 1950, when he joined the firm of Kenway Saddle & Leather. The owner, Kenneth R. Coppick, had a keen interest in history, and published a monthly magazine, *The Canadian Cattleman*. In 1950, Eagle Tail wrote an article for the magazine, entitled "Canada's First Cattleman – The Indian."[10] It contained seven portraits by him, while the cover featured a full-sized image of a Blackfoot named Calf Child.

BELOW: *Dick Knight, a member of Big Plume's band of Sarcees, shows his individual style of dressing his hair. He was photographed in the early 1920s.*

EAGLE TAIL CONTRACTED pneumonia during the Calgary Stampede and died on July 22, 1951, at the age of fifty-seven. Eagle Tail's step-grandson remembers going to the rooming house after the funeral. "After he died," he recalled, "my mother and granny went through his stuff. I saw lots of things there. There were letters from England and all kinds of beadwork. Granny kept some of it but I don't know what happened to the rest."[11] Some of the beadwork was later sold to the Luxton Museum, in Banff, Alberta, Canada, while other items simply disappeared without trace. Eagle Tail's former employer, Ken Coppick, arranged to buy the entire photographic collection of some 1,100 negatives from his widow and held the negatives for a number of years. He then donated them to the Luxton Museum and from there they were transferred to the Glenbow Museum in Calgary, where they reside today.

EAGLE TAIL IS REMEMBERED as having "lots of cameras,"[12] and this is borne out by examining the existing collection. Most of the portraits were taken with a professional camera using 4 x 5 inch (10 x 13cm) cut film, while others were taken with a camera using a slightly smaller

Alberta, but he is still remembered fondly. "I think he was pretty good to the Sarcee people," concluded a step-grandson.[13] In addition, his photographs remain a legacy to his dedication to preserve part of a culture that he loved and admired, and tried to adopt as his own.

---

NOTES

1. There are some discrepancies regarding the names of some employers and dates of employment, so the annual Calgary City Directories have been used as the sole source.

2. Interview with Fred Eagletail, October 4, 1998.

3. *Ibid.*

4. Arnold Lupson, *The Sarcee Indians of Alberta*. Calgary: Phoenix Press, 1923, 16pp., illus.

5. *Ibid.*

6. Taken from the expression, "I wanna be an Indian," it has been used to describe people who dress in Indian costume, dance, and otherwise pretend that they are Indians.

7. Interview with Fred Eagletail, October 4, 1998.

8. *Ibid.*

9. Interview with Gordon Crow Child, May 21, 1997.

10. *Canadian Cattleman*, July 1950, pp.7, 14.

11. Interview with Fred Eagletail, October 4, 1998.

12. *Ibid.*

13. *Ibid.*

# THE SARCEE

## A BRIEF HISTORY

THE SARCEE INDIANS, who have lived on a reserve on the southwestern outskirts of Calgary, Alberta, since 1881, were allies of the Blackfoot but were always a distinct and independent tribe. They were originally part of the Beaver, or *Tsattine*, tribe that inhabited the forested area north of the North Saskatchewan River. As the southernmost band of this tribe, the Beavers tended to dwell in the present Edmonton area, hunting on the plains during the summer months. However, when the Cree Indians, armed with guns supplied by traders, penetrated westward from Hudson Bay early in the eighteenth century, they drove a wedge between the two tribes. The Beavers moved north, deeper into the woodlands of the Peace River area, while the Sarcees became a separate tribe and migrated on to the plains. They were at war with the Crees who had displaced them, so they became allies of the Blackfoot against their common enemy.

In 1790, trader Edward Umfreville referred to them as "a small tribe which has separated from the main body, and now harbor in some country about the Stony [Rocky] Mountains, where they keep to themselves."[1] The Sarcees explain their split from the Beavers through a legend. According to the story, the entire tribe was crossing a large lake in midwinter when a woman noticed an animal's horn protruding from the ice. When she struck it with an axe to break it free, the ice cracked and the tribe was split into two groups, one going north and the other south. The origin of the name "Sarcee" is unknown. In their own language, they are the *Tsuu T'ina*, meaning "earth people," implying they once had been as plentiful as grains of soil. However, their

LEFT: *To show how children's costumes imitated those of their parents, Eagle Tail photographed Roger and Patsy Runner in front of a decorated tepee in the 1930s.*

numbers were never large, ranging between 250 and 500 people in the nineteenth century. They often hunted alone, but in times of danger they joined Blood and Blackfoot bands in search of buffalo. There was some intermarriage, but the Sarcees never lost their identity or their language. They became bilingual, using their own language within their camps and speaking Blackfoot to their allies and fur traders.

They were described in 1811 as "the bravest tribe in all the plains, who dare face ten times their own number."[2] For example, in the early 1860s the Sarcees were engaged in a fight with a party of Crees on the Battle

River. Although outnumbered and driven back during the first onslaught, they rallied under the leadership of their chief, Bull Head, and succeeded in routing their enemy. Partly because of this event, Bull Head was subsequently recognized as a great chief. In another

*BELOW: Crow Collar was one of the leading holy men in the Sarcee*

... discovered a number of

... and killed him, and later ...

thirty battles, killed five enemy, took two scalps, and captured many horses. He ultimately became head chief of the tribe.

*ritual at the Sun Dance.*

Even young boys took part in raids against their enemies. One Sarcee recalled: "When I was ten years of age I accompanied two older warriors to Montana in order to steal horses from our enemies. We came upon an encampment of Dakota Indians, and by the light of the moon I stole among their tents and drove off four horses."[3] The next day, the trio was found by their pursuers. The boy was surrounded but when the Sioux saw how young he was, they let him go. He returned to his own land on foot where he discovered his friends had returned safely with the stolen horses.

## SARCEE WAY OF LIFE

The tribe, although small, was divided into bands, or family groups. By the late nineteenth century these included the Blood band, under Big Plume; the Broad Grass band, under Crow Child; the Aloof People, under Crow Chief; the Uterus band, under Old Sarcee; and the Young Buffalo Robes, under Many Horses. They often traveled and hunted together, but in the spring they separated to search for game, to renew their tepee poles, and to replace their worn lodge covers. They traveled far out on to the open plains, and in early summer they joined together or camped with one of the Blackfoot or Blood bands to hold a Sun Dance. In the autumn they moved to the foothills, where they sometimes used buffalo jumps or empoundments to kill large numbers of animals. The meat was sun

LEFT: *Three Sarcee women wear dresses typical of their tribe in the 1930s. On the left is the widow of Old Man Spotted. Next to her are Mary Big Belly and her mother, Maggie. The woman on the left, being the eldest, wears the most traditional dress with a curved design at the top.*

dried, pulverized, and mixed with dried berries and hot fat to make a food called "pemmican," which was stored in leather bags and could be preserved and eaten during the winter months. The Sarcees remained

or as long as the buffalo herds were close

LEFT: *Five prominent Sarcees were photographed as they prepared for the Calgary Stampede parade in the 1920s. Left to right are: unknown; Jack Big Plume; Big Knife; Fox Tail; and Tom Heaven Fire. Note that Big Knife's horse has a type of face mask which, as in the past, provided protection during battle.*

LEFT: *Pat Grasshopper is seen here in full regalia at the Calgary Stampede in the 1920s. Born in 1866, he witnessed the great treaty between his people and the Canadian government in 1877, and was recognized as the historian of the Sarcee tribe.*

RIGHT: *Big Knife was a leading ceremonialist in the Sarcee tribe during the 1920s. He was custodian of the tribe's most important Medicine Pipe Bundle, reciting prayers for it each morning and evening. He is seen here, seated in front of his tepee and wearing a buffalo horn headdress.*

made a clearing on the ice where they played a whipping game. Each boy found a round stone to use as a pin top. He had a braided whip to make it spin and called out to his friends that he was a warrior. Another boy got his top spinning and crashed it against his opponent's rock, so that one "warrior" attacked the other. The winner gave a loud war whoop and took possession of the loser's stone. At other times, boys and girls slid down slopes on sleds made of buffalo ribs, while in the spring they had mud fights. In the latter game, two teams faced each other, all armed with long willow sticks with mud balls fastened to the ends. As they drew closer, they used the stocks to propel the mud balls at their "enemy" until one team finally fled.

Winter was the time to gather prime buffalo robes, as well as the pelts of wolves, foxes, and coyotes. Some of these were used for making clothing, while others were taken in spring to Hudson's Bay Company trading posts at Rocky Mountain House or Fort Edmonton. The Sarcees visited the trading posts twice a year – once in the spring, with the results of their winter hunts, and again in the autumn, when they traded horses and dried meat for European goods such as axes, knives, kettles, guns, and blankets. As the Hudson's Bay Company settled along the North Saskatchewan River, the Sarcees moved southward to avoid conflict with Crees and Metis, who often accompanied the traders. By the mid-

BELOW: *Persons taking part in the Sarcee Beaver Medicine Bundle ceremony are seated inside the lodge. The wife of* Walking in the Water *is seated at the center.*

nineteenth century, they ranged primarily along the Red Deer and Bow rivers and in 1855 they were described as "British Indians, who neither hunt or trade on American soil."[4] By this time they had shed any semblance of a woodland existence and were entirely Plains

1869, American traders began bringing huge supp Canada, debauching the Sarcees and Blackfoot and causing great havoc among them. In response, the North-West Mounted Police were sent to the West in 1874 to introduce law and order. Three years later, the Canadian government negotiated Treaty Number Seven with the tribes of southern Alberta. Signing for the Sarcees was Bull Head as head chief, with Many Horses, Drum, and Eagle Robe as minor chiefs. The population of the tribe was estimated at that time to be 255 persons. The treaty provided that the Sarcees give up their hunting grounds in exchange for a reserve and assistance in hunting and farming. At first, the tribe was expected to share a common reserve with the Blackfoot, but the Sarcees wanted their independence. They were allies of the Blackfoot but not such good friends that they wanted to live with them. In protest, they left the reserve and pitched their tepees on the outskirts of the village of Calgary. In the early winter of 1880, they began to starve and almost burned down a local trading store when demanding food. In panic, local police called for help, and the government decided to move the Indians to the headquarters of the Mounted Police at Fort Macleod, where they would keep an eye

LEFT: *Joe Big Plume, head chief of the Sarcee tribe from 1920 to 1946, was Eagle Tail's brother-in-law. He stands in front of his bullrush tepee, holding a pipe-tomahawk decorated with war designs. According to tradition, pipe-tomahawks could be smoked in times of peace, or used as weapons in war.*

on them. A detachment of thirty police arrived in near blizzard conditions, and when the Indians refused to move, their lodges were torn down. With no alternative, they departed from Calgary in

near Calgary. This is where Indian Edgar Dewdney found them in the summer of 1881. Exasperated, the official finally gave the Indians what they wanted: a reserve consisting of three townships of land southwest of Calgary. Two years later, the tribe signed a new treaty with the Canadian government, setting out their reserve "to have and to hold the same unto the use of the said Sarcee Indians forever."[5]

The Sarcees were prairie buffalo hunters and had never known any form of agriculture, but in order to survive they had to turn to farming. The early efforts were more like gardens than they were fields. By 1884 they had only twelve acres (4.8 hectares) under cultivation, where they grew about thirty bushels of potatoes, turnips, and barley. After the transcontinental railway line passed through the area, Calgary developed into the large town which offered employment prospects for the Sarcees. Some Indians made a living selling berries, wood, hay, and Christmas trees in town, while others worked on nearby ranches, branding cattle and breaking horses. Yet there was a dark side to their

ABOVE: *Maggie Big Belly proudly exhibits her beadwork, horse gear, and finery at the Calgary Stampede's Indian village. At that time the Sioux-type eagle feather headdress was worn purely as decorative headgear. Only later did it take on a religious significance for men.*

proximity to a major community, for members of the tribe fell prey to bootleggers selling illicit whiskey, white men seeking native girls, and persons ready to victimize them at every turn. In spite of these problems, the Sarcees clung to their old way of life, but at the same time progressed in agriculture and in making a living.

Anglican missionaries became established on the reserve in 1886 and opened a school in the same year, but during the next ten years there were only three conversions to Christianity. As one missionary commented, "To understand the difficulties to be contended with in dealing with the Sarcees, it must be remembered that they are more tenacious of their customs and superstitions than other Indians. Until recently they believed themselves doomed to extinction in the near future, and did not appear to wish to exert themselves to avoid what they considered to be their inevitable fate."[6] Most Sarcees were quite comfortable with their own religion, which was based upon the power of the Sun spirit, and the existence of holy protectors, which took the forms of creatures such as deer, otters, and eagles.

In 1896, a few Sarcees purchased cattle and soon developed a ranching industry. Young Sarcees found that, unlike farming, raising cattle had many similarities to their old way of life. The cattle, like the buffalo, wandered in search for food, and Indian cowboys, with their horses, traveled with them. Within a few years, many Sarcees became proficient horsemen and took part in rodeos and stampedes. Within the reserve, the Sarcee tried to preserve their old ways. They continued to speak the Sarcee language, and some even remembered the Blackfoot tongue and used it when visiting neighboring reserves. They held annual Sun Dances, bought and transferred medicine bundles (a collection of objects and materials which were thought to

RIGHT: *A Sarcee dances with a sacred otter skin during ceremonies which take place during the opening of a Beaver Medicine Bundle. This bundle, containing animal and bird skins and other objects, was believed to have originated with the Sun spirit.*

be endowed with spiritual powers), made painted tepees, and treasured other religious objects. They buried their dead above ground, usually in coffins placed in small cabins or on hills from which point the spirits of the deceased could come and go.

One of the most serious problems for the Sarcees occurred early in their reserve years, when overcrowding in small, ill-ventilated houses caused an outbreak of tuberculosis. In 1896 there were thirty deaths and only twelve births on the reserve. By 1920, the situation had become so serious that a doctor was appointed Indian agent and the reserve was virtually transformed into a sanitarium. Even the school was closed after a government official noted that "All the children except four show the presence of tuberculosis in a state that requires active attention . . . the children are now fighting a losing battle with this dread disease."[7] The program had good results, and from a population of 160 in 1924, the tribe grew gradually to more than 800 in 1998.

During Eagle Tail's time, the old men of the Sarcee tribe wore woollen coats, breechclouts, and leggings. Old women had dark clothes, shawls,

LEFT: *Maggie Big Belly sits on the grass in front of her cabin with her two grandchildren. On the left is Fred Eagle Tail and on the right is May Eagle Tail.*

kerchiefs, and brightly beaded belts with attachments carrying awls for sewing, and steels for sharpening knives. All wore moccasins, and in winter a heavy blanket completed their garb. Their hair was left long and was braided for special occasions. Younger men and women tended to follow the dress of their white counterparts. Men dressed

housing development, gravel company, golf course, and service stations. They have their own schools, cultural museum, and sports center, and sponsor annual rodeos and Indian Days. In short, the Sarcee Indians of today have found that delicate balance between their distinctive native culture and survival in a modern technical world.

NOTES

1. Umfreville, 1954:103

2. Henry and Thompson, Coues ed., 1897, Vol. 2:737

3. Jenness, 1938:4

4. Doty, 1966:25

5. *Indian Treaties and Surrenders from 1680 to 1890.* Ottawa: King's Printer, 1950, vol.2, p.136.

6. *Annual Report of the Department of Indian Affairs for the Year 1895.* Ottawa: Queen's Printer, 1896, p.78.

7. "Copy of Dr. Corbett's Report on the Sarcee School," Calgary Indian Mission Papers, M1356/f.6, Glenbow Archives, Calgary.

# THE SARCEE

## MATERIAL CULTURE
## AND LIFESTYLE

ALTHOUGH THE LIFESTYLE of the Sarcee was similar to that of the tribe to which they became most closely associated – the Blackfoot[1] – several distinctive traits remained when Eagle Tail married into the tribe in the 1920s. Foremost was their language which, although belonging to the widely used Athapascan linguistic stock, was so complex that few, if any, outsiders ever mastered it. Perhaps less apparent at this time would be a physical difference between the two tribes. That such a distinction existed was reported on in the 1880s, when one observer recorded that the "Sarcees do not strike me as so fine or tall a race as the Blackfeet."[2] Some forty years later, the Blackfoot themselves were still said to describe the Sarcee as *sokh-siu*, meaning "short people." Nevertheless, by this time the extensive intermarriage that had taken place between the two tribes, extending over several generations, largely made this description obsolete. Certainly Eagle Tail's (and other) photographic records appear to show very similar physical characteristics for both tribes.[3]

While seemingly greatly influenced by the Blackfoot in religion, ceremonies, costume, and mythology, a closer examination indicates there were several distinctive ethnic markers, probably due to the Sarcee's apparent difficulty in accepting the very highly ritualized aspects that were such an important feature of the Blackfoot world view.[4] Several painted tepee designs, as will be discussed, were distinctively Sarcee, and the attitudes toward the concept of power differed considerably, the Sarcee emphasis being on a display of generosity rather than a deep belief in the ancient Algonquian world view as held by the

RIGHT: *Sarcee Indians painting a tepee cover. The top and bottom of the cover is embellished with conventional designs. The central area is painted with more specific motifs. The three men are (left to right) Joe Big Plume, Bull Collar, and Pat Grasshopper.*

Blackfoot.[5] Furthermore, in contrast to the Blackfoot, by Eagle Tail's time the complex and traditional ritual transfer of painted tepee designs was replaced by simple inheritance of the designs to close [illegible][6] Th[illegible] while the Sarcee did adopt much of Blackfoot [illegible] much [illegible] ready accommodation, largely unrestrained by religious or previous cultural constraints, underlines tribal ethos. A willingness to adopt new

ideas — to change, appropriate, and explore, but still maintain their tribal integrity and solidarity — is a distinguishing characteristic of the Sarcee.

## THE PAINTED SARCEE TEPEE

Eagle Tail's photographs show Sarcee dwellings which, at first glance, closely resemble those of the Blackfoot. There were, however, some significant differences, not only in the variation of painted designs, but also in the way the Sarcee viewed the significance of the designs and the obligations associated with them. Several of Eagle Tail's insightful photographs show the various steps in the production of a Sarcee tepee and the techniques of painting, erection, and internal furnishing. In early days, a traditional tepee was fabricated of ten to fourteen tanned buffalo hides. However, by the reservation period in about 1880, and with the virtual extinction of the buffalo, covers were made of trade canvas. There were several advantages in the use of such material: canvas was more lightweight and therefore more easily transported than buffalo hide (as a result, tepees tended to be larger in Eagle Tail's time). In addition, canvas tepees were more translucent, so tended to be brighter and more airy inside.

ABOVE: *Sarcee Indians painting the conventional design of earth and "fallen stars." On the left in the foreground is Old Sarcee and on the right is Dick Starlight Senior.*

When laid out, a tepee cover is almost semi-circular in shape, with cut-outs and apertures at the smoke hole and door. The main painting was generally carried out by several skilled assistants, who were instructed on the nature of the symbolic designs by the owner; final details might be

34

completed after the erection of the tepee itself. A four-pole base was generally used by both the Sarcee and Blackfoot, some fourteen further poles being stacked around to produce a conically shaped frame. The cover was then put into place (below) by tying its upper

LEFT: *Putting the cover on the tepee pole base. The cover was attached to the top of one of the poles and then raised, as shown here. The cover was then pulled around the conical framework and laced up the front. Small stakes were driven through holes or loops at the bottom of the cover, so anchoring it to the ground.*

the air space between it and the main cover ensured that it was warm in winter and cool in summer. These linings were generally decorated either with pictographic records of the war and hunt drawn by the men or, as shown below, with neat geometric designs generally produced by the women. Although largely gone unrecorded, there is some evidence to suggest that these geometric designs were highly symbolic and the exclusive property of the woman who drew them or the guild to which she belonged.

Additional furnishings were in the form of beds and backrests made of willow

LEFT: *Maggie Big Belly painting the interior tepee lining with geometric designs. Notice that she is smoking a briar pipe. The tepee linings reduced drafts and improved circulation, removing smoke from the fire.*

sticks, which were supported on tripods. Tastefully embellished with beadwork and colored cloth at the top and sides, these were ideal tepee furnishings, being lightweight and easily transported by simply rolling them up and stacking them on the travois. Travois were the means by which the nomadic equestrian Plains tribes transported both

LEFT: Eagle Tail's wife, Maggie, sitting inside her tepee. Note the tepee liners decorated with geometric designs and the tepee backrests to her left and right. Such backrests served as a type of chair during the day and a bed at night.

LEFT: *Display of Sarcee beadwork inside a tepee. The beadwork was produced by Maggie Big Belly.*

RIGHT: *A tepee cover fixed around the conical frame. Here, slim, pointed sticks, about 12 inches (30cm) in length are pushed through holes in the front of the covers, lacing the edges together. Decorative patterns were often carved on the sticks.*

beadwork, quillwork, and painted hides hung up over cords adjacent to the colorful tepee lining (above). Almost without exception, painted Sarcee tepee designs never showed the Maltese Cross-like figure that was an important feature of most Blackfoot tepee designs.[8] Such an omission underlines the Sarcee's relative independence from several Blackfoot religious concepts – they never fully adopted the Algonquian world view. Certain respected Sarcee individuals acquired, through a dream, tepee designs that were unlike any found in Blackfoot designs, suggesting instead inspiration from ancient times when the Sarcee roved with the Plains Cree. Through his wife, Maggie Big Belly, Eagle

Tail inherited such a tepee design. Referred to as the "Peace-pipe Tepee," it was one of four which Big Belly, a highly successful Sarcee medicine man, acquired in a dream from a mystical snake.[9]

Other tepee-like structures used by the Sarcee and Blackfoot, as well as several

ABOVE: Stacked poles producing a war or hunting lodge-type configuration. Eagle Tail's encampment c.1930. Poles arranged this way were used by war or hunting parties as temporary shelters.

hunting expeditions. Vital to the success of the party, their location was well known and appear to have been repaired and used many times.[10]

## THE CYCLE OF SARCEE LIFE

As one ethnologist observed more than sixty years ago, the Sarcee child entered the world "nameless, but generally not without honour."[11] The child was considered a precious gift from the "Great Spirit" and the

LEFT: *Maggie Big Belly in the process of tanning a hide. Hide tanning was a laborious, time-*

*a cord or pole (as shown here).*

parents often approached a woman known for her kindness, honesty, and warm heartedness to bless the baby. Traditionally, she did this by holding the child's right hand and with deep conviction saying something like "May the kindliness and charity I feel towards others animate you also." A name was bestowed upon the child by a person of high standing – a medicine woman or man, or perhaps a highly successful warrior; a name obtained in a vision was particularly valued. Unlike the Blackfoot, there was no religious purification ceremony involving the use of the sweat lodge, and a moss bag instead of a hard board cradle was generally used to carry the child (left).

Up to the age of nine or ten, both girls and boys were strongly under the influence of their mother. Then it changed markedly for the boy, who

FAR LEFT: *Winnie Bull, Sarcee Indian, photographed in the early 1920s. Winnie was born in 1892, and her baby Elsie is being carried in a moss bag. Moss bags are a distinctive northern style of child's cradle, a link with the Sarcee's sub-Arctic heritage.*

LEFT: *Mrs Maggie Big Belly drying and smoking meat on a stick over a fire. Note the trade kettle hanging from the tripod over the fire. These were much favored trade items being produced in England and France.*

was taken under firm control by his father and enrolled as a member of his band. In the nineteenth century, the emphasis was on training for the warpath and the hunt, but in Eagle Tail's time (the 1920s to 1940s) it became more important for boys to learn about tribal ceremonies and customs, and to learn to be a caring member of the

tobacco to make kinnikinik.[12]

LEFT: *Mrs Old Man Spotted, Sarcee Indian, drying bearberries (Uva-ursi) to mix them with other plants and tobacco to make kinnikinik. The term "kinnikinik" derives from the Algonquian meaning "what is mixed": there were at least six different varieties, depending on the locality.*

Not all was work in a Sarcee encampment, however, and even on non-festive occasions, something was usually stirring. At dawn, elderly people wandered to the hilltops to pray, while boys and young men rounded up the horses and had their morning swim in the river. Men might be seen embellishing their robes with pictographic figures referring to days of past glory, others singing while in the throes of transferring a medicine bundle. As the day moved on, camp life became rich in variety, and many pastimes and distractions were available as well as the more serious pursuits. One was gambling by both sexes: dice ("four sticks") or the hand-game ("hidden sticks") were, and indeed still are, the most popular. The wheel and arrow game was also very popular (below left). Here, a small hoop with beaded spokes was bowled

LEFT: *Two Sarcee Indians playing the game of wheel and arrow on the Sarcee reserve c.1920. In this game, which involved both skill and chance, the wheel was bowled against some obstacle, as it fell each opponent thrust an arrow through it; the score was given according to its position relative to the spokes.*

against an obstacle and as it fell, arrows from opposing sides were thrust through it. Although many such games were largely ones of chance, they did require some skill, and several men and women were recognized for their expertise in certain games.

LEFT: *Maureen Big Plume, daughter of Joe Big Plume, taken at the Calgary Stampede Indian Village in the 1920s. The pony is gracefully caparisoned with a soft tanned deer or elk skin, which is held in place by the rider on the saddle and the beaded martingale across the pony's chest.*

mundane – ploughing, pulling wagons, and transporting wood. On several occasions throughout the year, however, earlier days of glory were re-enacted in parades at the Calgary Stampede and when certain rituals such as the Sun Dance and Beaver Bundle ceremonies took place. Caparisoned horses and the old-style mode of transportation, the travois, were then much in evidence (right). So too was traditional costume. Some men proudly exhibited regalia that was more fitting to the buffalo days of the previous century, and wore old-style costume, such as Yellow Lodge (far right), dressed in a heavily porcupine-quilled buckskin shirt.

ABOVE: *Dick Starlight Senior, Sarcee Indian, wearing a fur hat with buffalo horns and riding a horse with the long poles of the travois dragging along the ground.*

In the 1920s, heavily beaded garments were popular, exhibiting complex patterns in both the overlaid and lazy stitch. Although geometric patterns predominated, floral designs were also relatively popular and – something certainly due to white influence – even beaded ties were worn. Old-timers too, although lacking elaborate regalia, could show off certain personal achievements, such as in the case of Big Plume, with his particularly long scalp-lock braid.

Eagle Tail photographed several women in colorful regalia. For example, he photographed Mrs Big Knife wearing a straight-up style headdress of eagle feathers, embellished with strips of rawhide bound with porcupine quills, a beaded headband, brass bells, and fringes of ermine skins. Such headdresses were obviously adopted from the Blackfoot, and were strongly associated with the men's Horns Society,

LEFT: *Yellow Lodge, a Sarcee Indian, wearing a quilled shirt and carrying a pipe-tomahawk. The shirt*

*the front is a modern feature.*

LEFT: *Mrs Old Sarcee, photographed c.1927. She is wearing a flaring-style eagle feather headdress, which was adopted from the Sioux after days of inter-tribal warfare. Although structurally identical to the Sioux headdress, the additional decoration – spots of ermine on the feathers and the beaded browband – are distinctively Sarcee.*

RIGHT: *Old Mrs Big Plume, mother of chief Big Plume and of Maggie Big Belly. Note the interesting design of beadwork on her dress and that the lower part of the cape is fringed with large "basket" beads threaded on buckskin thongs.*

although they were sometimes worn by women. Less traditional is the costume of Mrs Old Sarcee (above) — a warbonnet of eagle feathers adopted from the Sioux and strictly, if tradition was adhered to, worn only by high status warriors. The mother of Joe Big Plume (right), chief of the Sarcee from 1922 until 1941, however, wears more traditional costume for the period: a heavily beaded dress, worked in the overlaid stitch and fringed with buckskin thongs. Her kerchief, however, does not identify her tribally — it was widely used throughout the Northern Plains at this time.

## RELIGION AND CEREMONIES

While by Eagle Tail's time white
contact had considerably modified
early religious beliefs of the Sarcee, it

perhaps even intan
as rock and stone. Vision quests and
dreams were believed to reveal these
sources of power and perhaps endow a
long life, immunity in hazardous
circumstances (such as in the hunt or
war), or the ability to heal sickness.
Above all, the Sarcees saw man not as a
special creation divorced from the rest
of nature, but very much an integral
part of it. It was considered that by
association with creatures or objects
endowed with desirable powers such as strength, intelligence,
endurance or longevity, specific abilities could be acquired. These
abilities could lead to success in the hunt or on the warpath — even in
love. Charms or medicine-objects were considered a manifestation of
these powers; they came as gifts from successful individuals or were
purchased often with detailed instructions as to their use and the
associated obligations. Much of the Sarcee ritual centered around the

sweat lodge, for it was believed that prayers offered in the lodge were communicated more directly to the higher powers. The nature of the fireplace where the stones were heated varied depending on the particular ceremony — the Sun Dance, Beaver Medicine Bundle (page 50), and Pipe Medicine Bundle, for example, demanded different-shaped fireplaces, varying number of stones, as well as distinct ritualistic procedures and ceremonial accoutrements.

LEFT: *Two Guns and his wife opening the Beaver Bundle, c. 1920. Note the two pipes on the ground. In the background, left to right, are Old Sarcee, Tom Many Horses, and David One Spot. Associated with such bundles was a special ceremonial headdress, which was worn by the woman who gave the Sun Dance; unfortunately, this headdress appears to have disappeared by the time Eagle Tail joined the tribe.*

LEFT: *Sarcee Medicine Pipe Bundle suspended from a wooden frame and standing outside the tepee. These*

NOTES

1. Strictly, the North Blackfoot or Siksika.

2. Wilson, 1888:248

3. Nevertheless, in 1929 a member of the Tims family, who were associated with the Sarcee for years, stated "Any who have seen the tall, stalwart Blackfoot and the short, stocky Sarcee side by side, will at once recognize the aptness of the [Blackfoot] name." (Tims, 1929:7) I have, however, found it difficult to resolve this observation.

4. Honigmann, 1956:17

5. Derived, in part, from the use of certain tepee designs or the ownership of medicine bundles. As Geertz (1973) explains, a "world view" of a particular group is its picture of the way things are. It is a concept of self, society, and nature. The world view of the Blackfoot (Algonquian) differed sharply from the Sarcee.

6. Brasser, 1991

7. *Ibid.*

8. Painted at the top and back of the tepee, it was symbolic of the Morning Star, who was considered a herald of the Sun.

9. Jenness, 1938:73

10. Such shelters, long since fallen into disuse, are still to be found in remoter parts of the Central and Northern Plains and have been visited by the author.

11. *Ibid*:18

12. This is derived from Cree or Chippewa (Algonquian) and means "What is mixed."

# THE BLACKFOOT

## A BRIEF HISTORY

FOR MANY YEARS, the name "Blackfoot" has been associated with the famous Indian tribes of the West. Together with the Sioux, Cheyenne, and Apache, they have gained the reputation of being fierce and independent warriors. As early as 1841, Sir George Simpson, Governor-in-Chief of the Hudson's Bay Company, spoke of them as a people "who have excited more curiosity than any other of the native tribes of North America." The Blackfoot nation is made up of four separate tribes, all sharing the same culture and language. These are the Blackfoot proper, or *Siksikah;* the Blood Indians, or *Kainai;* the North Peigans, or *Aputohsi-pikuni;* and the South Peigans, or *Amiskapi-pikuni.* Collectively, they are known as the *Saukwetapix* or "Prairie People." An ancient name for themselves was *Nitsitapix,* or "Real People," but today this is used to describe Indians generally.

Recent archaeological investigations reveal that the Blackfoot can trace their residence in southern Alberta back at least to 1550. According to Blackfoot mythology, the trickster/creator *Napi,* or the "Old Man," made the first people at the beginning of time. When he made men and women, they at first lived in separate camps, but he convinced them to unite, and the first marriages took place at Women's Buffalo Jump near the Porcupine Hills of Alberta. The antiquity of Blackfoot occupancy also is implied in the name of the Oldman River, one of the main watercourses through their hunting grounds. It is derived from the Blackfoot name *Napiotsi-kaxtsipi,* or "Where the Old Man Gambled," and a boulder monument paying tribute to the event existed for many generations on the upper waters of the Oldman. In

RIGHT: *Paul Little Walker, seen here, was an unusual man. He started life as a wild rebel, but became an Anglican lay reader after having a vision in which he said he visited heaven. He also became chief of the Blackfoot, and participated actively in the affairs of the tribe.*

1792, the site was visited by Hudson's Bay Company trader Peter Fidler, who described the layout of stones and wrote: "On my enquiring concerning the origin of this spot, the Indians gave me surprising & ridiculous account. They said that a White man (what they universally call Europeans) came from the South many ages ago, & built this for the Indians to Play at, that is different nations whom he wished to meet here annually & bury all animosities betwixt the different Tribes, by assembling here & playing together. They also say that this same person made the Buffalo, on purpose for the Indians.

BELOW: *This camp at the Calgary Stampede in the 1930s displays some of the richness of Blackfoot tepee designs. In the foreground are two horse travois.*

They describe him as a very old white headed man & several more things very ridiculous."[1] The reference to the old man, of course, was to *Napi*, not a white man. It fits very well with an account of *Napi*'s journey north from what is now Wyoming after the Big Flood, creating animals, birds, humans, and natural features of the land as he traveled.

was the basis of much of their religion. In 1811, Alexander Henry the

LEFT: *These are buffalo bones, unearthed from kill sites by Blackfoot Indians. They were used during the war for making explosives. Eagle Tail photographed this reminder of earlier days at the Gleichen railway station, near Calgary, in 1943.*

Younger, fur trader for the North West Company stated, "In summer they chase buffalo on horseback, and kill them with the bow and arrows, and in winter they take them in pounds."[2] Artist George Catlin said in 1832 that the Blackfoot follow "the immense herds of buffaloes, as they range over these vast plains . . . for the purpose of killing and drying buffalo meat which they bring in from their hunts, packed on horses' backs, in great quantities; making *pemmican*, and preserving the marrow-fat for their winter quarters . . . and make their long and tedious winter tolerable and supportable."[3]

ABOVE: *Annie Royal, photographed on the Blackfoot Reserve in the 1930s. Annie's grandmother was reputed to have been a white woman, who had been kidnapped from a family in Montana in the 1880s.*

The Blackfoot used the buffalo meat for food and the skins for clothing, lodges, bow cases, and knife sheaths. They also used rawhide to make containers, the thick necks of the bulls to make shields, hair was used for cushions, horns for spoons, hoofs for glue, sinew for bows, ribs for scrapers, bones for handles, and tails for fly brushes. The Blackfoot had several effective methods of hunting buffalo. The most productive was through the use of a buffalo jump, or *piskun*, where the buffalo were stampeded over a cliff and were either killed outright by the fall or dispatched by hunters as soon as they landed. A corral at the bottom of the jump prevented any animals from escaping. Another form of trapping buffalo was with the use of an impoundment or corral. A third method was when a man covered himself with a wolf or calf skin and managed to crawl close enough to the buffalo herd to kill sufficient animals to satisfy his own needs.

In addition to buffalo, the Blackfoot also hunted deer, moose, antelope, elk, mountain sheep, and mountain goats, both for their meat and skins. Antelope and deer skin, in particular, were preferred for men's and women's clothing. Smaller animals, such as porcupines, rabbits, and ~~[illegible]~~ ~~[illegible]~~ other food was scarce. Ducks,

*design tepee with members of his family. Left to right are Hilda, Gabriel, Violet, and Anne.*

LEFT: *This is a distant view of the Blackfoot Sun Dance camp in the 1920s. The religious ceremonies were taking place at the time in the brush structure in the center of the circle.*

collected for food. Cold-blooded creatures, such as fish, frogs, snakes, and lizards were shunned. The Blackfoot gathered wild turnips and camas (nutritious roots), as well as berries — Saskatoons, chokecherries, and bull berries, for example — which were dried and used in pemmican. They also made use of lodgepole pine for tepee poles and travois, vegetable and mineral compounds to make paint, porcupine quills for decoration, stone for projectile points, knives, and mauls, and clay for creating crude pottery pieces.

Horses were obtained by the Blackfoot in about 1730, and gave them a mobility

LEFT: *Duck Chief was head chief of the Blackfoot tribe. In this photograph, he wears an 1877 treaty medal*

which they had never before experienced. Instead of traveling five or six miles (8 to 10km) on a good day's journey, they now could travel fifteen to eighteen miles (24 to 29km). This meant they could more easily pursue the buffalo herds, travel to berry patches, and gather roots or other necessities over a much broader range. At the same time, they could accumulate and transport many more personal possessions. And warfare, which had previously been conducted for territorial protection, now became a means of seeking glory and wealth.

## CONTACT WITH EUROPEANS

The first European trading posts were established on the edge of Blackfoot country in the 1790s, and changed the annual cycle of the tribes. Previously, the Blackfoot had trapped only to provide furs for clothing for their own needs, but now these became a valuable commodity. In addition, they began drying meat in vast quantities to sell to the trading companies. Accordingly, their annual movements were changed to provide for visits to trading posts on the North Saskatchewan River in the spring and autumn.

A devastating effect of contact with Europeans was the spread of diseases which had previously been unknown to the Blackfoot and for which they had no immunity. Even relatively minor ailments, such as measles and scarlet fever, resulted in a high mortality rate. For example, a winter count for 1819 is remembered as "Coughing epidemic," relating to a measles outbreak which wiped out a third of the Blackfoot nation. Similarly, the 1864 winter count refers to "Black smallpox," when an

ABOVE: *Teddy Yellowfly, who was half Chinese, was a leading chief of the Blackfoot tribe in the 1930s. Well-educated, he traveled to several parts of North America representing his people. He was believed to have been murdered by a fellow Blackfoot in 1950.*

epidemic of scarlet fever killed more than 1,100 persons from the Blackfoot nation. But the worst killer was smallpox. According to Blackfoot winter counts, it first struck the tribe in 1764, just a few years after first contact. The next reference was in the winter count of

disease" and half the tribe

contact with European

expedition. In 1806, when the expedition was returning from the Pacific coast, it became involved in an altercation on the Two Medicine River in the present State of Montana, and two Peigans were killed. For the next twenty-five years, any white persons coming up the Missouri River were considered to be enemies. To make matters worse, the Americans had a different method of fur gathering than the British. While the British Hudson's Bay Company encouraged Indians to trap and bring the pelts to their trading posts, the Americans used the "rendezvous" system. This meant that white trappers went into Indian hunting grounds, where they trapped beaver and other animals and, at the same time, avoided any contact with the local Indians. Then, once a year, they

*Dance, it is believed that everyone's songs and prayers will go via this pole into the sky and to the Sun spirit.*

LEFT: *Pretty Young Man, who was photographed by Eagle Tail at the Calgary Stampede in 1927, wears the snake horn headdress of his tribe. The horn is buffalo and the cap is covered with weasel skins.*

gathered at a rendezvous point, such as Jackson Hole, Wyoming, where merchants brought their goods and exchanged them with the trappers for supplies, whiskey, and cash. Not surprisingly, any American trappers who entered Blackfoot country were considered to be invaders and thieves, and were killed as a result.

*Blood Sun Dance. Half the lodge will be painted black to symbolize night and half red for day. The holy men will go through a sweat bath to purify themselves before the main Sun Dance ceremonies.*

Americans and the Blackfoot. A year later, Fort Peigan was built at the confluence of the Missouri and Marias rivers, in the heart of Blackfoot country. From that time on, the Blackfoot successfully pitted British against European American traders, always looking for the best goods and the most competitive prices.

## GOVERNMENT INVOLVEMENT

In 1855, the United States government concluded a treaty with the South Peigan branch of the Blackfoot nation, giving the tribe a huge reserve and the promise of food and implements in exchange for giving up their hunting grounds. However, a decade later the government decided the reserve was too large, and after pressure from white settlers it made new treaties in 1865 and 1869. Although never ratified, these treaties reduced the reserve to a fraction of its original size. Further cuts were made through executive orders in 1873 and 1874, and by agreements in 1888 and 1895.

North of the border, the ownership of British territories in the west was transferred to Canada in 1869, but authorities had no means of enforcing law and order after the withdrawal of the Hudson's Bay Company. Accordingly, enterprising European American merchants discovered that they could operate within the legal vacuum of the Canadian prairies, selling whiskey and repeating rifles to the Blackfoot. In 1873 it was estimated that six hundred barrels of liquor were traded to the Blackfoot, and that between 1868 and 1873, twenty-five percent of the tribe died as a result of alcohol consumption and drunken brawls. Finally, the North-West Mounted Police were organized by the Canadian government, and in 1874 they were sent to the region to put down the illicit traffic.

FAR LEFT: *A young boy, Steven Many Fires, carries a holy shield while it is being transferred in a*

LEFT: *One of the most important rituals at the Blackfoot Sun Dance is performed by The Sacred Horn Society, seen here in 1927. Often, photographers were not permitted to record this ritual, so Eagle Tail may have been doing so without the knowledge of the society.*

LEFT: *After the holy women have performed their four-day ceremonies, all objects used by them are left as offerings to the Sun spirit. These include rocks from the fireplaces, poles from the lodge, cloth, and other items. These remain as sacred offerings for many years.*

Mounted Police, the Blackfoot willingly signed the treaty even though they did not fully understand the terms. Through this treaty, they surrendered their hunting grounds of approximately 50,000 square miles (129,500sq km) in Canada in return for reserves, annual treaty payments, and other amenities. Each of the three tribes — Blackfoot,

In their daily lives, most Blackfoot continued to speak their own language and retain important elements of their religion. In the 1920s and 1930s, the years in which Eagle Tail photographed members of the tribe, they were still holding their annual Sun Dance, performing Medicine Pipe dances, and supporting secret societies — all in the face of hostility from missionary organizations and government officials. Following World War II and the introduction of television, there was a gradual loss of language and cultural practices, but these have been partially offset by native-run colleges, which include Blackfoot history and culture as part of their programs.

LEFT: *The Indian on the left, He Will Be Black, and four ceremonialists, prepare to enter the Blackfoot Sun Dance lodge, c.1927.*

LEFT: *In 1939, King George VI and Queen Elizabeth (now Queen Mother) greeted Blackfoot leader Duck*

NOTES
1. Fidler, 1792: Entry for December 31
2. Henry and Thompson, Coues ed., 1897, Vol.2:530
3. Catlin, 1913, I:49

# THE BLACKFOOT

## MATERIAL CULTURE
## AND LIFESTYLE

THE BLACKFOOT RESERVE closest to Eagle Tail's adopted people, the Sarcee, was occupied by the Algonquian-speaking *Siksikah* or Blackfoot proper, situated on the Bow River and some fifty miles to the east of the Canadian city of Calgary, Alberta. Much reduced by devastating foreign diseases, such as smallpox and measles, their population at the time Eagle Tail knew them would not have exceeded one thousand. To the south were the other Blackfoot tribes, the Peigan, or *Pikuni,* and the Bloods, or *Kainai.* Eagle Tail's photographs suggest that sometimes he also visited these tribes, recording details of the popular and widespread Grass Dance, below, probably performed

BELOW: *A performance of the Grass Dance at the Blood Indian Sun Dance encampment, c.1940. Referred to by the Blackfoot as Kaspa, the Grass Dance, a mainly social dance, was widespread across the Plains by the 1890s.*

as a type of war-dance in inter-tribal warfare days after returning from the enemy. He also captured the highly religious Sun Dance (above) and even, during a Blood Indian gathering near Fort Macleod, the use of a dog travois (page 72.)

On occasions he crossed the border into the United States to visit the largest of the Blackfoot reserves in northern Montana, and occupied mainly by the South Peigan. Here, he met the well-known Bull Plume family, photographing them in all their finery; it is a study that tells us much about the changing styles of Blackfoot ceremonial regalia. It is clear that at times Eagle Tail and his wife, Maggie, followed the ancient pattern of the Blackfoot, as described by the ethnologist, John Ewers, as "truly international people, who make frequent journeys back and fourth (sic) across the line to visit friends and relatives on the other

ABOVE: *Preparations for transferring the ownership of medicine bundles during the Blood Sun Dance. Here, men and women are being painted before the ceremony takes place. Note the Maltese Cross at the top of the tepee. This symbolizes Morning Star, considered to be a great source of power.*

side."[1] Earlier contacts with such tribes as the Kiowa and Kiowa-Apache were also still apparent. Thus, Eagle Tail's photograph of the distinctive Blackfoot tepee (page 74), commonly known as the "hugging bear" tepee, documents a design which relates to the Kiowa-Sarcee-Blackfoot interaction in the latter years of the eighteenth century. At this time, and prior to their move to the Southern Plains, the Kiowa and Kiowa-Apache occupied southeastern Montana and the nearby Black Hills. Here, they had friendly intercourse with both the

RIGHT: *The South Peigan, Bull Plume and his wife and possibly his granddaughter. As a woman of high status, Mrs Bull Plume wears an ancient style of straight-up headdress.*

LEFT: *Dog pulling a travois. This was probably taken at a Blood Indian gathering near Fort Macleod in southern Alberta, Canada. Goods were transported like this by the Blackfoot before the use of the horse. The A-shaped drags were harnessed to the wolf-like dogs, who could drag up to 50 pounds (23 kilos). Travel by this means was both slow and tiresome.*

LEFT: *Painted tepee which belonged to the Blood Many Fires photographed by Eagle Tail in the 1930s. Such paintings were an expression of Blackfoot religious concepts and mythology, each painting being replete in symbolism. For obvious reasons, it was often referred to as the "hugging bear" tepee design.*

Blackfoot and Sarcee; one tepee design which the Kiowa adopted was a "hugging bear" type motif – very close to that which both the Blackfoot and Sarcee used.[2] The Blackfoot lifestyle Eagle Tail recorded was in many ways similar to that of the Sarcee – indeed, the

*Sarcee parents ... she married into the Blackfoot tribe. A good deal of intermarriage occurred between the Blackfoot and Sarcee, which tended to give rise to many common cultural traits. Here, Mrs Good Rider is pounding dried meat, probably to prepare "pemmican."*

## BLACKFOOT LIFESTYLE

The Blackfoot tribes with whom Eagle Tail came into contact had a long history of dominance of the Northern Plains. Of Algonquian linguistic stock, their origins can be traced back to the forests of the Northeast. Prior to the acquisition of the horse, the Blackfoot hunted their principal game – buffalo, elk, or pronghorn antelope – on foot, with stone or bone-headed arrows and spears. On occasions, a whole village worked together to lure a herd of buffalo to and over the edge of a steep bank or cliff edge; some such sites were used for several thousand years (see page 56.) The enormous buffalo has been described as "a veritable general store for the Indian,"[3] from which was derived nourishing food, skins for the construction of a tepee and clothing, and a variety of raw materials – horns, bones, hoofs, hair, and sinew – utilized in the manufacture of tools, weapons, household utensils, and many other useful articles.

This "stone age" lifestyle was probably relatively peaceful, since there was little cause for war – no surrounding tribes had possessions which the Blackfoot could not obtain in their own country. Pitched battles between large forces were therefore rare, and although on occasions there were clashes, loss of life was minimal. The aged Peigan chief, Saukamappee, described an encounter between Blackfoot and Shoshone which occurred around 1725 in the vicinity of the Eagle Hills (in present-day Saskatchewan, Canada). Armaments consisted of shock weapons, such as stone-headed war clubs and lances. Most warriors carried 5 foot (1.5m) long bows with flint-tipped arrows. Shields made of heavy rawhide were some 3 feet (1m) in diameter. Even with such protection, several men were wounded on both sides; night, however, quickly put an end to the battle and not a scalp was taken by either side "and in those days such was often the result."[4]

RIGHT: *Spotted Eagle's tepee c.1930. In early days, only a small number of tepees in a Blackfoot encampment had painted designs. Geometric designs made reference to sky and underwater powers. Animal figures – eagle, deer, otter, buffalo, and as here, horse – were highly impressive. The band from the mouth to the heart was referred to as the "heart line." The heart and the kidneys, in particular, were said to be the sources of power of the animals depicted.*

## A SOPHISTICATED STONE AGE

The acquisition of horses around 1730 dramatically changed Blackfoot lifestyle and, not surprisingly, Blackfoot mythology and religious concepts were quickly adapted to accommodate this unique single-toed creature. At the time of the first white contacts in the eighteenth century, the Blackfoot owned a great number of horses which they had obtained from tribes to the south. By the mid-nineteenth century, they became particularly noted for their immense horse herds – some distinguished individuals might own several hundred.

The advent of the trader — the first of whom entered Blackfoot territory in the eighteenth century — also brought great changes to Blackfoot culture.[5] Without question, on many counts life was made easier, and certainly lives were materially enriched; but the new property brought problems — old skills were lost, and the Blackfoot became increasingly dependent upon trade goods, such as knives, guns, ammunition, metal kettles, trade steels, axes, tomahawks, and trade cloth. Additionally on offer was an almost endless variety of baubles and beads, which considerably changed decorative and ceremonial accoutrements and costume. Such goods traveled virtually halfway around the world to get to the Blackfoot. Thus, there were mirrors and bells from Leipzig in Germany, colored ribbons, cloth, and calicos from England and France, and a vast variety of beads from Venice, Italy.

The newfound mobility, leisure-time, and luxury goods dramatically changed lifestyles in the fields of warfare, arts and crafts, trade, and ceremony. Religious concepts were challenged, too, as zealous missionaries – Catholics, Methodists, and Anglicans – did their best to convert the "heathens" to Christianity. It was not long before the Blackfoot (and indeed other Plains tribes) were utterly confused. However, many

RIGHT: *The Blackfoot, Water Chief at the Calgary Stampede, probably in the 1930s. Water Chief's gun is encased in a buckskin scabbard, beautifully beaded (with a traditional Blackfoot motif) and heavily fringed.*

tribes made an effort to accept all branches of Christianity as one ethnologist commented, "because they didn't know which was right, and they said that they were not going to take any chances."[6]

The effect of the the acquisition of the gun in about 1750 was that the Blackfoot became restless, aggressive, and a largely predatory people. Smaller tribes, such as the Sarcee and Gros Ventre *(Atsina)*, lived under Blackfoot protection, but others such as the Cree and Assiniboin to the north and east, the Sioux and Crow to the south, and Flathead and Kutenai to the west, were traditional enemies with whom they were almost constantly at war. Whites were grudgingly tolerated. The Peigan in Montana had little time for the United States Army, while the Blackfoot and Blood Indians managed to maintain a somewhat unpredictable friendship with the Hudson's Bay Company. A "safety valve" for the Blackfoot was the virtually boundless Canadian Plains. When pressures became too great they could retreat and continue with their ancient ways — unlike many of the other Plains tribes, such as the Sioux and Cheyenne to the south, who had no such land resource available. Largely for this reason, warfare with the United States was never extensive; not until the buffalo numbers began to dwindle in the 1880s, when many Blackfoot literally starved to death,[7] did the Blackfoot really see the need to negotiate for reserves and to abandon their nomadic lifestyle.

## TRADITIONS AND CEREMONIES

Despite the decline toward the end of the nineteenth century, days of past glories long remained with the Blackfoot in Eagle Tail's day, such

ABOVE: *Tom Turned Up Nose, c. 1930. His elaborate costume consists of an eagle feather headdress with ermine skin drops and a beaded shirt to which is attached a bronze treaty medal. Note the U-shaped pouch with crossed United States flag motifs.*

as evidenced by the impressive image of Water Chief in all his finery, (page 79) which not only underlines the preeminent place of the horse and gun in Blackfoot (and other Plains tribes) culture, but displays medals presented by visiting representatives of Queen Victoria, who ⟨illegible⟩ ⟨illegible⟩ esteem – a sentiment which

performed with great ⟨illegible⟩

LEFT: *Blackfoot medicine bundles were generally suspended from tripods, as shown here, and during the course of the day moved around the tepee so as to always be facing the sun, which was considered a great source of power.*

sacred medicine bundles, which were generally hung on a tripod of poles adjacent to the tepee (see page 81). Many Blackfoot bundles were individually owned, with payment being made to the bundle owner for use in the particular ceremonial associated with it. Sacred objects continued to be transferred with much traditional ritual and ceremony, while participation of young people ensured that such traditions – particularly the songs and important sequence of events – were passed down to successive generations.

Ancient fraternities, both women's and men's, still rigorously participated in the

BELOW: *An episode in the transfer of a medicine shield to the Blackfoot Indian, Raw Eater in the Blackfoot Sun Dance camp in the 1920s. The boy wears a feathered trailer and breechclout and has traditional long braids.*

Sun Dance, such as the Old Women's Society (right) and the Horn Society, the latter wearing traditional, sacred, straight-up headdresses (see page 84) and carrying enormous lances, generally crooked at the top. Legend leads to the assumption that these crooked lances have associations with food-gathering by women.[8] Certain individuals were also still to be seen wearing highly symbolic regalia, such as fringed shirt and leggings, a single horn headdress, and weasel and fur fringe. Others, such Big Crow, a Blood Indian, displayed elaborate hairstyles embellished with various shells, bone hairpipes, trade cloth, and

ermine, together with the adornment of symbolic face paint (page 85).

The annual Sun Dance, together with the festivals and activities of the organized societies, ensured that the gatherings never lacked thrills and were (and indeed still are) always full of interest and variety. Like the Sarcee, the Blackfoot enjoyed several gambling games, generally accompanied by the throbbing of a drum. The stakes were horses, weapons, sometimes even the participant's very clothes. Materially, the popular and widespread wheel and arrow game was just as hazardous; counts were usually in multiples of five, small pebbles being used as counters. The betting was by pledging a blanket for so many pebbles,

LEFT: *Big Crow, also
known as Spider, a
Blood Indian
photographed in the
1940s. He has an*

*beads, to which are
attached ermine tails
and a hand mirror.*

LEFT: *The Blackfoot headmen, Calf Child, Wolf Chief, and Red Leggings, at the Sun Dance in the 1920s.* gathering.

a knife for so many, and so on.[9] With their rich equestrian history, the Blackfoot continued to covet horses even though the days of nomadism were over. Thus, such annual summer events as the Calgary Stampede created the opportunity for nostalgic displays, with "make believe" warriors (below), costumed in warrior regalia and

LEFT: *Chief Buffalo Child Long Lance, Calgary 1928. He was an honorary blood brother of the Blackfoot.*

TOP RIGHT: *Mrs Dan Bull Plume wearing a straight-up headdress. The technique of fabrication of this particular headdress differs from the old style and probably had little sacred symbolism, in contrast to the earlier version.*

BOTTOM RIGHT: *Evelyn Brass, daughter of Big Old Man, Blackfoot, c.1927. She wears an elaborately beaded buckskin dress and her moccasins and ankle bands are decorated with seed beads.*

headdresses, proudly riding their finely caparisoned horses and reenacting past days of glory, real or imaginary.

## TRADITIONAL BLACKFOOT REGALIA

[...] [...] of the Blackfoot was replete in

[...]

[...] beadwork [...]

fringes, and colored cloth inserts, which are edged with beadwork on the skirt. Much is still of traditional style, however, resembling dresses made at least half a century earlier.[12] The costume of Mrs Dan Bull Plume, a South Peigan woman (top right) is, however, less traditional. Although her straight-up headdress resembles the old Blackfoot style, the way the feathers are laced to the headband shows outside – probably Sioux – influence, and her dress cape is embellished with cylindrical glass beads, some of which are more than 1 inch (2.5cm) in length; such beads did not come into use until the very end of the nineteenth century.

European cloth, introduced in about 1750 to the Blackfoot, caused a gradual displacement of clothing made of deerskin and buffalo, particularly after the 1890s, when game became scarce. Colorful clothing, which was made from English "point blankets"[13] as early as 1750, and traded to the Northern

LEFT: *Tony Crowchild, a Blackfoot Indian who was born in Billings, Montana, and died in December 1941 at the age of 89. Particularly impressive is the eagle feather headdress with the enormous flare; he also carries an eagle fan in his left hand. Note the necklace made of brass plates from old northwest guns.*

Plains Indians, is illustrated in the costume of Jack Big Plume (page 12.) Identical to that worn by the Blackfoot tribes they generally exhibited red, green, or yellow stripes on a white background. These *capotes* were ideal for wearing on the warpath —particularly on the so-called Horse Raids.[14]

changes in Blackfoot society.

---

NOTES

1. Ewers, 1952:7

2. Brasser, 1979: 34–35

3. Ewers, 1952:10

4. Thompson, 1916:328–329

5. Lewis, 1942

6. Ewers, 1971:141

7. Ewers, 1952:49

8. The author, in company with Hugh Dempsey, was privileged to recently visit a Horn Society gathering in southern Alberta. Much of the superb traditional regalia had been borrowed from museums and was subsequently returned. This was, apparently, an annual arrangement.

9. Wissler, 1911:60

10. Wissler, 1912, 1918. Taylor, 1993 and 1998

11. Orchard, 1916. Bebbington 1982. Taylor, 1994a.

12. Wissler, 1910. Ewers, 1945. Conn, 1961. Feder, 1984. Taylor, 1997

13. These were manufactured in Witney, England. The "points" (stripes) refer to the blanket size.

14. Ewers, 1955:183

15. These styles have been recently described and contrasted in some detail by the author in a study of actual specimens and earlier literature (Taylor, 1994b).

# THE STONEY

## A BRIEF HISTORY

THE HUNTING GROUNDS of the Stoney Indians in the nineteenth century ranged from the lofty heights of the Canadian Rockies, to the rolling foothills, and on to the buffalo plains of Alberta, Canada. Their name is derived from the term *Assinipwat*, meaning "stone people," which is also the source of their other name, the Assiniboin Indians. They were once part of the great Sioux nation, but they separated from their parent tribe near the Great Lakes in the 1600s and became allies of the Cree. By the 1700s, they had migrated west to the Rocky Mountains, where they found excellent hunting and trapping along the foothills. There they divided into several small bands, some spending their entire time peacefully in the foothills and woodlands, while others ventured on to the plains where they became buffalo hunters and warriors. The first white man to meet these Rocky Mountain Stoneys was Anthony Henday, a Hudson's Bay Company explorer from the Isle of Wight, England, who entered their camps in the autumn of 1754 and spent the winter with them. When the first trading posts were built on their lands in the 1790s, the Stoneys proved to be excellent beaver trappers and hunters. In 1811, fur trader Alexander Henry the Younger described Stoney men as "generally of moderate stature, rather slender, and very active" and that they were "most hospitable to strangers who arrive in their camps."[1]

In defense of their lands or in raiding enemy horse herds, the Stoneys often fought neighboring tribes, such as the Kootenays, Blackfoot, and Shuswap. They were described as "fierce fighters and mighty hunters, possessing great physical courage and stoical endurance, qualities

RIGHT: *George Maclean, whose personal name was Walking Buffalo, was educated in a mission school and later became chief of the Bearspaw band of Stoney Indians.*

which all men admire, and which characterize all great peoples."[2] Most of their adventure stories relate to warfare or hunting. For example, on one occasion, when scouts reported a camp of thirty Blackfoot lodges near Chief Mountain, a war party under Left Hand swept down and killed everyone except for two young men who managed to escape

FAR LEFT: *Stoney woman and child. The Stoney still hunted and fished in the foothills of the Rockies long after moving to their reserve.*

This incident occurred in 1877, when the Stoneys were camped at Blackfoot Crossing to sign a treaty with the Canadian government. Their hunters had just killed a number of buffalo and left one old bull standing alone and confused. Bearspaw's father handed the boy a gun and told him to shoot it. Resting the heavy weapon on his father's shoulders, the boy pulled the trigger and the recoil hurled him to the ground. When he stood up, his shoulder was badly bruised but the buffalo was dead.

## THE THREE BANDS

During the 1860s and 1870s, the Stoneys along the Rocky Mountains were divided into three bands, each named after its

RIGHT: *The Banff Indian Days, seen here in the 1930s, was a summer tourist festival sponsored by local merchants. In 1978, the tribe pulled out of the annual event and began to organize their own Indian Days on their reserve.*

LEFT: *Ben Kaquitts was a prominent Stoney leader who rejected life on the reserve and moved to a site in the foothills known as the Kootenay Plains. In the 1940s, the Canadian government finally gave Kaquitts and other families their own reserve in that area.*

RIGHT: *When Joshua and William Hunter were born, twins were such a rarity in the Stoney tribe that they became known as Joshua and William Twin. They worked as guides during the construction of the Canadian Pacific Railway in the 1880s, and actively participated in the Banff Indian Days.*

chief. In the southern part of their hunting grounds were the Bearspaw band, which often hunted buffalo on the open plains far south into Montana. North of them, was the Chiniki band near the present Banff National Park, while in the woodlands on the upper reaches of the North Saskatchewan River was the Goodstoney band. The latter two bands sometimes pursued buffalo but more often hunted moose, deer, and elk. They also trapped porcupines, rabbits, and marmots, and fished the many lakes and streams that dotted their hunting grounds. The kidneys and livers of larger animals were highly valued as food,

and often eaten raw. Special delicacies were boiled moose nose soup, roasted buffalo tongues, and cooked beaver tails.

The average Stoney tepee, designed to hold a single family of eight, was smaller than those used by the nearby Blackfoot tribes. It was often made of moose hide, although members of the Bearspaw band preferred buffalo hides. Tepees used between ten and sixteen poles; three poles were bound together as a tripod, and the other poles were laid against it. Two more poles were used to control the air vents, or ears, at the top of the tepee; these poles slipped into tiny pockets in the ears. In this way, the ears could be shifted to control the draft and the smoke.

## STONEY CHRISTIANITY

The Stoneys were the first tribe in the region to accept Christianity. They were visited by Methodist missionary Robert Rundle in 1841 and two of their most prominent leaders, Tchakta and Twoyoungmen, became converts. A few years later, when the Earl of Southesk was hunting along the foothills, he was surprised to hear some Stoney Indians singing hymns, even though there was no missionary present. "They are Christians," he observed, "having had some teaching from Protestant missionaries, and seem to be most religious, excellent people."[3] Southesk noted that in the evening, a bell was rung in the Stoney camp and a church service was held by the Indians in their own language, after which more hymns were sung. The first permanent Stoney mission was established in 1873 at Morley, on the Bow River just west of Calgary. Four years later, the Bearspaw, Chiniki, and Goodstoney bands then signed Treaty Number Seven with the Canadian government, and took a reserve near the mountains. At that time, the population of the reserve was estimated to be about five thousand. They were issued with tools in the hope that they would

RIGHT: *Flora was the wife of George Maclean, the Stoney chief who was better known as Walking Buffalo. She was a daughter of Hector Crawler, one of the most outstanding chiefs of the tribe.*

LEFT: *Sarah was the wife of traditional Stoney chief Jonas Twoyoungmen. Around her neck she wears a soumak necklace made of braided sweetgrass. These necklaces, with their aromatic odor, were popular among the Stoney people.*

LEFT: *David Bearspaw was a traditional chief of the Stoney tribe. When Eagle Tail photographed him, the*

become farmers but the soil was marginal and their reserve was subject to early frosts. Most Stoneys preferred to hunt in the foothills, as long as there was big game to be found. The Goodstoney band favored the Kootenay Plains area along the headwaters of the North Saskatchewan, and in 1892 one of its leaders, Peter Wesley, abandoned his reserve

LEFT: *George Crawler was dressed in the typical regalia of the Stoney tribe when photographed by Eagle*

While the Stoneys may have been isolated from trading posts and European settlement during the early years, this all changed in 1883, when the Canadian Pacific Railway passed through the middle of their reserve, to be followed many years later by the Trans-Canada Highway. As a result, visitors often dropped by to see the progress of the tribe. In 1895, for example, a reporter examined life on the Stoney Reserve, visiting the Indian agent's office, the slaughter house where rations were issued, the residential school, and individual homes. "Each adult is allowed a pound [of beef] a day and the children a proportionate amount," he said when he witnessed the Stoneys being rationed. "The cattle are shot at the slaughter house and hung up for half an hour to bleed, then skinned and cut up." He also noted that "the houses are neat, one storey log buildings, the logs squared and painted white, and the roofs generally shingled."[4]

In 1889, a washout on the Canadian Pacific Railway line stranded a large number of tourists at Banff National Park, so a contingent of Stoneys was invited to entertain the bored visitors. They camped in the park for

a week, offering horse races, foot races, tug-of-wars, parades, and dancing. So successful was the show that the Stoneys were invited to return for Queen Victoria Day and Dominion Day celebrations, and in about 1908 the Banff Indian Days became an annual festival, held in July immediately after the Calgary Stampede. Over the years, the event was a strong motivating force for the Stoneys to retain certain elements of their culture, such as beadwork, singing, and dancing.

Some of the prominent persons associated with the Indian Days were Hector Crawler, Walking Buffalo, John Hunter, Hanson Bearspaw, Joshua and William Twin, and Mark Poucette. In 1919, Edward, Prince of Wales, became one of the first persons honored by the tribe. He was made an honorary chief and given the name Morning Star. In

their situation improve. When Eagle Tail began visiting them in the 1920s, they were poor, suffered from inadequate health services, and were at the mercy of the Indian agent. Not until after World War II did the situation materially change, when natural gas discoveries on Stoney land provided a new base for economic development. But they have also suffered as a result of their reserve being on the main line of the Trans-Canada Highway, and sliced up by two major highways, a rail line, and power lines. A traditional and friendly people, they try to keep to themselves, but still participate in many cultural or tourist programs to which they are invited.

NOTES

1. Henry and Thompson, Coues ed., 1897, Vol.2:516–517

2. Parker, 1901

3. Southesk, 1875: 245

4. *Calgary Herald*, June 19, 1895.

# THE STONEY

## MATERIAL CULTURE
## AND LIFESTYLE

AS WE HAVE SEEN in the previous chapter, the extensive cultural history of the Stoneys finally led to the formation of three bands — Chiniki, Goodstoney[1] and Bearspaw — being settled in 1877, on a small reserve at Morley on the Bow River, approximately midway between Calgary and Banff in Alberta, Canada. These were the people with whom Eagle Tail came into frequent contact, the Sarcee Reserve where he married and settled with Maggie Big Belly being but a few miles to the east. Although linguistically unrelated (the Stoneys were Siouan, the Sarcee Athapascan), the two tribes had a good deal in common, both being considerably influenced by their earlier woodland/subarctic heritage. A major difference, however, was that while the Sarcee allied themselves with the Blackfoot and adopted, at least superficially, both their religion and ceremonial as well as material culture patterns, the Stoney were, traditionally at least, constantly at war with the Blackfoot and remained largely independent of their influence.

## THE STONEY TEPEE

The Stoney tepee differed significantly from that of the Sarcee and Blackfoot. Generally, they were smaller, unpainted, and had a three-pole base. The air vent flaps had small pockets, into which the tip of the two "smoke hole" poles slipped, while Blackfoot and Sarcee tepees had an eyelet in the flap, through which the tip projected. As Hugh Dempsey has observed, "this knowledge could be vital in times of war, for if a person stumbled upon a strange camp, he could immediately tell if they were friend or foe."[2] Reflecting also their hunting practices, several of the Stoney bands, such as the Chiniki and Goodstoney (as

RIGHT: *The Stoney Indian, George Crawler, mounted in full regalia. This was taken at the Calgary Stampede in the mid 1920s. The extensive use of star symbols on both the saddle blanket and horse collar are typical of Stoney decorative motifs at this time. Note the pockets in the ears of the smoke flaps, which is a distinguishing feature of Stoney tepees when compared with those of the Sarcee or Blackfoot.*

LEFT: *Sarah Twoyoungmen, wife of the Stoney tribal councillor, Jonas Twoyoungmen, demonstrates the technique of thin-slicing meat at the Banff Indian Days. She is wearing a kerchief which was, together with shawls or blankets, typical everyday wear for Stoney women at the time (1942).*

FAR RIGHT: *Sarah Twoyoungmen, c.1925. It was not unusual for Indian women to smoke women's pipes, which were generally small and elbow-shaped. That shown in this picture is clearly a white man's briar pipe obtained in trade.*

well as those such as the Alex and Paul who settled west of Edmonton, Canada), often used moose hides — instead of the widely used buffalo — for their tepee covers. These dwellings housed a typical family of eight persons. Such traditional, early tepees were, as has already been mentioned, generally smaller than the average buffalo hide Plains

subsistence pattern of existence that they were able to maintain for many years following the virtual extermination of the buffalo during the 1880s, during which other tribes — the Blackfoot and Sarcee to the east, for example — faced starvation.

The Stoney tepee was considered the property of the dominant woman of the household, and it was her responsibility to supervise its dismantling, erection, and efficient daily organization. Since fresh meat would soon spoil, a major activity was cutting the meat into thin slices – in a similar way to the preparation of bacon – and drying it in the sun. The ability to prepare meat this way was considered a particularly important

skill, and there was an air of friendly competition between households, when the meat was placed on the racks outside the tepees to dry.

While the organization of the tepee was traditionally the woman's responsibility, the painted designs, which became an important feature of a Stoney

recorded colorful, painted, large canvas tepees. Favored designs were discs, stripes, triangles, and diamonds with, at times, realistic renderings of horses, hunting, and household scenes. Although attractive, little, if anything, in these designs made reference to the traditional Stoney cosmos, unlike the painted tepees of the Blackfoot.

## THE STONEY SUN DANCE

Powerful and very traditional ceremonies were still practiced in Eagle Tail's time, in particular the Sun Dance, with its associated four-day rituals. This ceremony, possibly adopted from the semi-sedentary Mandan, who lived along the Missouri River, and subsequently modified by the Plains nomads, was reported on in some detail in the mid-nineteenth century by the fur trader Edwin Denig[3]. Referred to then as the "Sacred Lodge," it was described as the "greatest public or national ceremony" of the tribe. The events captured in Eagle Tail's pictures resemble those recorded by Denig almost three generations before: the cutting and raising of the central pole, accompanied by

FAR LEFT: *Blind Eagle, also known as Job Stevens. He is wearing a fur hat favored by Stoney men, since they spent much time considered to make good head-coverings. Blind Eagle carries a rawhide-covered drum and appears to have a small painted dance shield attached to his fringed shirt.*

FAR LEFT: *Prayers before the cutting of the center pole for the Stoney Sun Dance, Morley c.1930. The Stoney were the first*

*ceremonies.*

LEFT: *Scene from the Stoney Sun Dance, c.1950. Here, branches of trees are being stacked around and over the framework of the Sun Dance bower. The central pole, which is highly decorated with colored cloth offerings, supports part of the bower. Note the men on horseback bringing in the cut branches.*

men and women who "sing a kind of hymn or tune, though no words are used in it," the decoration of this pole, "painted and decked out very gaily," and the participants all "dressed in their very best raiment and the whole presents a lively and interesting appearance."[4]

Denig goes on to describe the bizarre self-torture that was a common feature of the ceremony. This was accomplished by cutting the breast with the knife horizontally, a "stout stick" might then be thrust through the incisions, and the penitent attached to the pole by a rawhide cord. Alternatively, the cords were attached to "three or four buffalo bulls' heads and horns . . . and they drag this weight over the ground." Denig concludes, "Nothing is eaten or drunk during all this time." It is clear from Eagle Tail's photographs that nothing quite so extreme as these tortures was practiced during his time. Clearly, the influence of Methodist ministers, who entered Stoney country as early as the 1840s, did much to modify the ceremony. Nevertheless, all evidence suggests that the Sun Dance remained the most important and most sacred of Stoney ceremonies well into the twentieth century.

## COSTUME OF THE STONEY

The abundance of fur-bearing animals in the wooded foothills and mountains of Stoney territory was an important source of clothing for the various members of the tribe. Beaver, bighorn sheep, and otter pelts[5] were used extensively to make robes and head coverings, while deer, wapiti, and moose were used to fabricate dresses, shirts, leggings, and moccasins. Decoration of these garments in the early days consisted of paint, porcupine quillwork, fringes of various furs, and hair; additional embellishments included horn, shells, and a variety of animal teeth, especially the milk teeth of the bull elk. Later, with the introduction of beads, costume decoration became more elaborate.

RIGHT: *Interior of the completed Sun Dance lodge. Here can be seen the main participants who, as one 1850s observer recorded, are "painted and decked out very gaily." Most appear to be blowing on whistles (probably made from eagle-wing bones), the shrill sound of which was believed to evoke the higher powers. This is one facet of a four-day ceremony which, in earlier times, until banned by the Canadian government, often included a self-torture episode.*

FAR LEFT: *Sitting Eagle, also known as John Hunter, in dress regalia consisting of an eagle feather warbonnet, beaded* [illegible] *was confined at the waist by a sash or belt.*

LEFT: *Red Cloud or Joshua Wildman, c.1930. Red Cloud's hairstyle, with long side braids and eagle feather, is typical for older traditional Stoney men at this time. He carries an elaborate dance staff – much favored by the Stoneys – and a broad band of beadwork is worn across his shoulder.*

LEFT: *Walking Buffalo, also known as George McLean, in ceremonial regalia. His headdress is made of mature golden eagle feathers, each tipped with ermine and horsehair and laced to a skull cap. A beaded brow band to the ends of which are attached large white, fluffy eagle feathers, completes the embellishments. Walking Buffalo's buckskin shirt is decorated with broad beaded bands over the shoulders, worked in the overlaid stitch. The bold patterns are typical of the Stoney for this time.*

At the height of their power in the mid-nineteenth century, the Stoney were distinguished by their fine ceremonial costume. Edwin Denig was of the opinion that their "own dresses of skins fancifully arranged, adorned with feathers, beads, shells, and porcupine quills, are much more highly prized by them than any article of dress of European manufacture introduced by the traders."[6] Denig notes that in the mid

the tails of two young golden eagles (24 feathers) cost "something more than a horse," as were ten ermine skins or one hundred elk teeth.

The costumes worn by the Stoneys photographed by Eagle Tail similarly display elaborations and the extensive use of raw materials, such as buckskin, fur, feathers, plumes, and rawhide. In addition, all costumes in Eagle Tail's time were embellished with colored seed beads, which were purchased at traders' stores. A well-known store – Luxtons, in Banff – seemingly had considerable influence on the type and color of the beads used by Stoneys during Eagle Tail's time. For this reason, examination of Stoney costume in the ethnological collections[7] revealed a predominance of orange, red, and yellow beads; particularly unusual was the use of these bright colors as a background – combinations which the Blackfoot seldom, if ever, used at this period. Another characteristic of Stoney beadwork is a decided tendency to run the lines of the beads along the long axis of the object being embellished – bags, belts, and knife sheaths, for example. This seldom, if ever, occurs in the beadwork of adjacent tribes, such as the Sarcee and Blackfoot. The use of non-traditional motifs in Stoney beadwork is also very apparent in Eagle Tail's photographs: floral designs, crosses, five-pointed stars, and unusual arrow-type motifs predominate. The inspiration for such designs was obviously varied; however, it is well documented that the Methodist church had a strong impact on Stoney culture and thought, and the Canadian Pacific Railway and the Trans-Canada Highway, which run through the middle of their reserve, exposed the Stoney people to a variety of external influences. Fortunately, the process of accommodation and assimilation resulted in something unique to these resilient and imaginative people.

Today, the Stoneys – particularly the Chiniki band – are active and enthusiastic in the production of craftwork, reflected in much of early twentieth-century costume, such as moccasins, knife sheaths, gauntlets, and belts. There are, however, some surprises: moving with the times, and in true Stoney spirit, at least one enterprising lady has imported the idea of yet another potentially popular item which had its origins more than two thousand miles to the east amongst the Algonquian Ojibwa . . . a dreamcatcher!

RIGHT: *Blacksmith, also known as Dan Wildman wearing a fine headdress made of golden eagle feathers. The style, which had its origins with the Sioux, was widely used on the Northern Plains from the late nineteenth century onward. The termination of the beaded brow band is unusual, being a rectangular beaded element. Note the buckskin collar and necktie, a Stoney innovation, inspired by the formal dress of the white man.*

---

NOTES

1. These were later renamed the Wesley band.

2. Dempsey, 1998:27

3. Denig, 1930:488-491

4. *Ibid*:488

5. A fine shirt in the Glenbow Museum, Calgary, is made of otter hides, fringed with ermine. Broad beaded bands, across the shoulders and down the arms, have patterns in bright red and yellow (specimen number AF.528.5A).

6. Denig, 1930:585

7. Studies of Stoney and Sarcee costume were carried out by the author at the Smithsonian Institution in Washington and at the Glenbow Museum in Calgary (1996 and 1998 respectively).

# INDEX

# BIBLIOGRAPHY

Bebbington, Julia M. 1982 *Quillwork of the Plains*. Glenbow-Alberta Institute, Calgary.

Brasser, Ted J. 1979 *The Pedigree of the Hugging Bear Tipi in the Blackfoot Camp*. In *American Indian Art*. Vol. 5. No.1., Scottsdale, Arizona.

1991 *The Sarsi: Athapaskans on the Northern Plains. Arctic Anthropology.* Vol 28 No 1

Catlin, George 1913 *North American Indians*

, James 1960 *A Visit to the Blackfoot Camps*. In *Alberta Historical Review*. No.14:3.

Ewers, John, C. 1945 *Blackfeet Crafts*. Dept. of the Interior, United States Indian Service, Haskell Institute, Lawrence, Kansas.

1952 *The Story of the Blackfeet*. Dept. of the Interior, Bureau of Indian Affairs, Haskell Institute, Lawrence, Kansas.

1955 *The Horse in Blackfoot Indian Culture*. Bulletin 159. Bureau of American Ethnology, Smithsonian Institution, Washington, D.C.

1971 *A Unique Pictorial Interpretation of Blackfoot Indian Religion in 1846-1847. Ethnohistory*. Vol.18.No.3. The American Society for Ethnohistory, Tempe, Arizona.

Farr, William E. 1984 *The Reservation Blackfeet, 1882-1945: A Photographic History of Cultural Survival*. University of Washington Press, Seattle & London.

Feder, Norman 1984 *The Side Fold Dress*. In *American Indian Art*. Vol.10.No.1. Scottsdale, Arizona.

Fidler, Peter 1792 *Journal of a Journey over Land from Buckingham House to the Rocky Mountains in 1792 & 3*. Hudson's Bay Company Archives, Provincial Archives of Manitoba, Winnipeg.

Geertz, C. 1973 *The Interpretation of Cultures* New York, Basic Books

Henry and Thompson (Alexander Henry and David Thompson) 1897 *New Light on The Early History of the Greater Northwest. The manuscript journals of Alexander Henry and David Thompson, 1799-1814*. Edited by Elliott Coues. 3 Vols Francis P. Harper, New York.

Honigmann, John J. 1956 *Notes on Sarsi Kin Behaviour*. In *Anthropologica*, No.2.

Jenness, Diamond 1938 *The Sarcee Indians of Alberta.* Bulletin No.90. *Anthro.* Series No.23. National Museum of Canada, Ottawa.

Lewis, Oscar 1942 *The Effects of White Contact upon Blackfoot Culture.* Centennial Anniversary Publication, The American Ethnological Society, 1842-1942. University of Washington Press, Seattle.

Lupson, Arnold 1923 *The Sarcee Indians of Alberta.* Phoenix Press, Calgary.

Orchard, William C. 1916 *The Technique of Porcupine Quill Decoration among the North American Indians.* Contributions from the Museum of the American Indian. iv,I., Heye Foundation New York.

Parker, Elizabeth 1901 *The Canadian Alps.* In *Calgary Herald.* July 25.

Southesk, Earl of 1875 *Saskatchewan and the Rocky Mountains.* Edmonston and Douglas, Edinburgh.

Taylor, Colin F. 1993 *Saam: The Symbolic Content of Early Northern Plains Ceremonial Regalia* (Bilingual Americanistic Books.) Dietmar Kuegler. Wyg auf Foehr, Germany.

  1994a *The Plains Indians.* Salamander Books Ltd., London.

  1994b *Wapa'ha: The Plains Feathered Head-dress (Die Plains Federhaube.)* Verlag für Amerikanistik, Wyk auf Foehr, Germany.

  1997 *Yupika, The Plains Indian Woman's Dress: an overview of historical development and styles.* (Bilingual, English/German.) Verlag für Amerikanistik, Wyk auf Foehr, Germany.

  1998 *Iho'lena. Voices from the past: messages for the future. Cultural, religious and military content of Plains Indian artefacts.* (Bilingual, English/German.) Verlag für Amerikanistik, Wyk auf Foehr, Germany.

Thompson, David 1916 *David Thompson's Narrative of his Explorations in Western America, 1784-1812.* Edited by J.B. Tyrrell. Toronto.

Tims, Winifred A. 1929 *The Interesting Origin of the Sarcee Indians of Canada.* In *The American Indian*, Vol.4.No.2. Tulsa.

Umfreville, Edward 1954 *The Present State of Hudson's Bay.* Ryerson Press, Toronto.

Wilson, Rev.E.F. 1888 *Report on the Sarcee Indians, Report: On the North-Western Tribes of Canada (1885-1889).* In *Report of the British Association for the Advancement of Science.* 58th Meeting, Bath.

Wissler, Clark 1910 *Material Culture of the Blackfoot Indians.* American Museum of Natural History. Vol.V., New York.

  1911 *Social Organization and Ritualistic Ceremonies of the Blackfoot Indians. Part I: The Social Life of the Blackfoot Indians.* American Museum of Natural History, New York. Vol.VII.

  1912 ditto. Part II: *Ceremonial Bundles of the Blackfoot Indians.* American Museum of Natural History, New York. Vol. VII.

  1918 *The Sun Dance of the Blackfoot Indians.* In *Anthro. Papers of the American Museum of Natural History.* Vol.XVI., New York, 1921.